name:

_____

school:

_____

And the merry love the fiddle,
And the merry love to dance.

~ *William Butler Yeats*

Irish Dance Feis Record Book
- preliminary & open champion -

~ Available on Amazon and Etsy ~

Copyright © 2011, 2015, 2017

Feisbooks

Record of Apparel
(size, vendor, date, comments)

soft shoes:

hard shoes:

socks/tights:

class costume:

solo costume:

wig/tiara:

boy tie/belt:

accessories:

Record of apparel
(size, vendor, date, comments)

soft shoes:

hard shoes:

socks/tights:

class costume:

solo costume:

wig/tiara:

boy tie/belt:

accessories:

Notes:

Feis Name: _____

Date: *Location:*   *Dancer #:*

COMPETITION	LEVEL/AGE	# DANCERS	COMMENTS	RESULTS
Soft Shoe				
Hard Shoe				
Set Dance				

COMPETITION	LEVEL/AGE	# DANCERS	COMMENTS	RESULTS
Championship				

SPECIALS	LEVEL/AGE	# DANCERS	COMMENTS	RESULTS

TEAMS	LEVEL/AGE	# TEAMS	COMMENTS	RESULTS

Notes:

Feis Name: _____

Date: _____ Location: _____ Dancer #: _____

COMPETITION	LEVEL/AGE	# DANCERS	COMMENTS	RESULTS
Soft Shoe				
Hard Shoe				
Set Dance				

COMPETITION	LEVEL/AGE	# DANCERS	COMMENTS	RESULTS
Championship				

SPECIALS	LEVEL/AGE	# DANCERS	COMMENTS	RESULTS

TEAMS	LEVEL/AGE	# TEAMS	COMMENTS	RESULTS

Notes:

Feis Name: _____

Date: *Location:*   *Dancer #:*

COMPETITION	LEVEL/AGE	# DANCERS	COMMENTS	RESULTS
Soft Shoe				
Hard Shoe				
Set Dance				

COMPETITION	LEVEL/AGE	# DANCERS	COMMENTS	RESULTS
Championship				

SPECIALS	LEVEL/AGE	# DANCERS	COMMENTS	RESULTS

TEAMS	LEVEL/AGE	# TEAMS	COMMENTS	RESULTS

Notes:

Feis Name: _____

Date: *Location:*   *Dancer #:*

COMPETITION	LEVEL/AGE	# DANCERS	COMMENTS	RESULTS
Soft Shoe				
Hard Shoe				
Set Dance				

COMPETITION	LEVEL/AGE	# DANCERS	COMMENTS	RESULTS
Championship				

SPECIALS	LEVEL/AGE	# DANCERS	COMMENTS	RESULTS

TEAMS	LEVEL/AGE	# TEAMS	COMMENTS	RESULTS

Notes:

Feis Name: _____

Date: *Location:*   *Dancer #:*

COMPETITION	LEVEL/AGE	# DANCERS	COMMENTS	RESULTS
Soft Shoe				
Hard Shoe				
Set Dance				

COMPETITION	LEVEL/AGE	# DANCERS	COMMENTS	RESULTS
Championship				

SPECIALS	LEVEL/AGE	# DANCERS	COMMENTS	RESULTS

TEAMS	LEVEL/AGE	# TEAMS	COMMENTS	RESULTS

Notes:

Feis Name: _____

Date: *Location:*   *Dancer #:*

COMPETITION	LEVEL/AGE	# DANCERS	COMMENTS	RESULTS
Soft Shoe				
Hard Shoe				
Set Dance				

COMPETITION	LEVEL/AGE	# DANCERS	COMMENTS	RESULTS
Championship				

SPECIALS	LEVEL/AGE	# DANCERS	COMMENTS	RESULTS

TEAMS	LEVEL/AGE	# TEAMS	COMMENTS	RESULTS

Notes:

Feis Name: _____

Date: Location: Dancer #:

COMPETITION	LEVEL/AGE	# DANCERS	COMMENTS	RESULTS
Soft Shoe				
Hard Shoe				
Set Dance				

COMPETITION	LEVEL/AGE	# DANCERS	COMMENTS	RESULTS
Championship				

SPECIALS	LEVEL/AGE	# DANCERS	COMMENTS	RESULTS

TEAMS	LEVEL/AGE	# TEAMS	COMMENTS	RESULTS

Notes:

Feis Name: _____

Date: _____ Location: _____ Dancer #: _____

COMPETITION	LEVEL/AGE	# DANCERS	COMMENTS	RESULTS
Soft Shoe				
Hard Shoe				
Set Dance				

COMPETITION	LEVEL/AGE	# DANCERS	COMMENTS	RESULTS
Championship				

SPECIALS	LEVEL/AGE	# DANCERS	COMMENTS	RESULTS

TEAMS	LEVEL/AGE	# TEAMS	COMMENTS	RESULTS

Notes:

Feis Name: _____

Date: *Location:*   *Dancer #:*

COMPETITION	LEVEL/AGE	# DANCERS	COMMENTS	RESULTS
Soft Shoe				
Hard Shoe				
Set Dance				

COMPETITION	LEVEL/AGE	# DANCERS	COMMENTS	RESULTS
Championship				

SPECIALS	LEVEL/AGE	# DANCERS	COMMENTS	RESULTS

TEAMS	LEVEL/AGE	# TEAMS	COMMENTS	RESULTS

Notes:

Feis Name: _____

Date: Location: Dancer #:

COMPETITION	LEVEL/AGE	# DANCERS	COMMENTS	RESULTS
Soft Shoe				
Hard Shoe				
Set Dance				

COMPETITION	LEVEL/AGE	# DANCERS	COMMENTS	RESULTS
Championship				

SPECIALS	LEVEL/AGE	# DANCERS	COMMENTS	RESULTS

TEAMS	LEVEL/AGE	# TEAMS	COMMENTS	RESULTS

Notes:

Feis Name: _____

Date: _____ Location: _____ Dancer #: _____

COMPETITION	LEVEL/AGE	# DANCERS	COMMENTS	RESULTS
Soft Shoe				
Hard Shoe				
Set Dance				

COMPETITION	LEVEL/AGE	# DANCERS	COMMENTS	RESULTS
Championship				

SPECIALS	LEVEL/AGE	# DANCERS	COMMENTS	RESULTS

TEAMS	LEVEL/AGE	# TEAMS	COMMENTS	RESULTS

Notes:

Feis Name: _____

Date: Location: Dancer #:

COMPETITION	LEVEL/AGE	# DANCERS	COMMENTS	RESULTS
Soft Shoe				
Hard Shoe				
Set Dance				

COMPETITION	LEVEL/AGE	# DANCERS	COMMENTS	RESULTS
Championship				

SPECIALS	LEVEL/AGE	# DANCERS	COMMENTS	RESULTS

TEAMS	LEVEL/AGE	# TEAMS	COMMENTS	RESULTS

Notes:

Feis Name: _____

Date: _____ Location: _____ Dancer #: _____

COMPETITION	LEVEL/AGE	# DANCERS	COMMENTS	RESULTS
Soft Shoe				
Hard Shoe				
Set Dance				

COMPETITION	LEVEL/AGE	# DANCERS	COMMENTS	RESULTS
Championship				

SPECIALS	LEVEL/AGE	# DANCERS	COMMENTS	RESULTS

TEAMS	LEVEL/AGE	# TEAMS	COMMENTS	RESULTS

Notes:

Feis Name: _____

Date: *Location:*   *Dancer #:*

COMPETITION	LEVEL/AGE	# DANCERS	COMMENTS	RESULTS
Soft Shoe				
Hard Shoe				
Set Dance				

COMPETITION	LEVEL/AGE	# DANCERS	COMMENTS	RESULTS
Championship				

SPECIALS	LEVEL/AGE	# DANCERS	COMMENTS	RESULTS

TEAMS	LEVEL/AGE	# TEAMS	COMMENTS	RESULTS

Notes:

Feis Name: _____

Date: *Location:*   *Dancer #:*

COMPETITION	LEVEL/AGE	# DANCERS	COMMENTS	RESULTS
Soft Shoe				
Hard Shoe				
Set Dance				

COMPETITION	LEVEL/AGE	# DANCERS	COMMENTS	RESULTS
Championship				

SPECIALS	LEVEL/AGE	# DANCERS	COMMENTS	RESULTS

TEAMS	LEVEL/AGE	# TEAMS	COMMENTS	RESULTS

Notes:

Feis Name: _____

Date: Location: Dancer #:

COMPETITION	LEVEL/AGE	# DANCERS	COMMENTS	RESULTS
Soft Shoe				
Hard Shoe				
Set Dance				

COMPETITION	LEVEL/AGE	# DANCERS	COMMENTS	RESULTS
Championship				

SPECIALS	LEVEL/AGE	# DANCERS	COMMENTS	RESULTS

TEAMS	LEVEL/AGE	# TEAMS	COMMENTS	RESULTS

Notes:

Feis Name: _____

Date: *Location:*   *Dancer #:*

COMPETITION	LEVEL/AGE	# DANCERS	COMMENTS	RESULTS
Soft Shoe				
Hard Shoe				
Set Dance				

COMPETITION	LEVEL/AGE	# DANCERS	COMMENTS	RESULTS
Championship				

SPECIALS	LEVEL/AGE	# DANCERS	COMMENTS	RESULTS

TEAMS	LEVEL/AGE	# TEAMS	COMMENTS	RESULTS

Notes:

Feis Name: _____

Date: _____ Location: _____ Dancer #: _____

COMPETITION	LEVEL/AGE	# DANCERS	COMMENTS	RESULTS
Soft Shoe				
Hard Shoe				
Set Dance				

COMPETITION	LEVEL/AGE	# DANCERS	COMMENTS	RESULTS
Championship				

SPECIALS	LEVEL/AGE	# DANCERS	COMMENTS	RESULTS

TEAMS	LEVEL/AGE	# TEAMS	COMMENTS	RESULTS

Notes:

Feis Name: _____

Date: *Location:* *Dancer #:*

COMPETITION	LEVEL/AGE	# DANCERS	COMMENTS	RESULTS
Soft Shoe				
Hard Shoe				
Set Dance				

COMPETITION	LEVEL/AGE	# DANCERS	COMMENTS	RESULTS
Championship				

SPECIALS	LEVEL/AGE	# DANCERS	COMMENTS	RESULTS

TEAMS	LEVEL/AGE	# TEAMS	COMMENTS	RESULTS

Notes:

Feis Name: _____

Date: Location: Dancer #:

COMPETITION	LEVEL/AGE	# DANCERS	COMMENTS	RESULTS
Soft Shoe				
Hard Shoe				
Set Dance				

COMPETITION	LEVEL/AGE	# DANCERS	COMMENTS	RESULTS
Championship				

SPECIALS	LEVEL/AGE	# DANCERS	COMMENTS	RESULTS

TEAMS	LEVEL/AGE	# TEAMS	COMMENTS	RESULTS

Notes:

Feis Name: _____

Date: *Location:*   *Dancer #:*

COMPETITION	LEVEL/AGE	# DANCERS	COMMENTS	RESULTS
Soft Shoe				
Hard Shoe				
Set Dance				

COMPETITION	LEVEL/AGE	# DANCERS	COMMENTS	RESULTS
Championship				

SPECIALS	LEVEL/AGE	# DANCERS	COMMENTS	RESULTS

TEAMS	LEVEL/AGE	# TEAMS	COMMENTS	RESULTS

Notes:

Feis Name: _____

Date: *Location:*   *Dancer #:*

COMPETITION	LEVEL/AGE	# DANCERS	COMMENTS	RESULTS
Soft Shoe				
Hard Shoe				
Set Dance				

COMPETITION	LEVEL/AGE	# DANCERS	COMMENTS	RESULTS
Championship				

SPECIALS	LEVEL/AGE	# DANCERS	COMMENTS	RESULTS

TEAMS	LEVEL/AGE	# TEAMS	COMMENTS	RESULTS

Notes:

Feis Name: _____

Date: *Location:*   *Dancer #:*

COMPETITION	LEVEL/AGE	# DANCERS	COMMENTS	RESULTS
Soft Shoe				
Hard Shoe				
Set Dance				

COMPETITION	LEVEL/AGE	# DANCERS	COMMENTS	RESULTS
Championship				

SPECIALS	LEVEL/AGE	# DANCERS	COMMENTS	RESULTS

TEAMS	LEVEL/AGE	# TEAMS	COMMENTS	RESULTS

Notes:

Feis Name: _____

Date: _____ Location: _____ Dancer #: _____

COMPETITION	LEVEL/AGE	# DANCERS	COMMENTS	RESULTS
Soft Shoe				
Hard Shoe				
Set Dance				

COMPETITION	LEVEL/AGE	# DANCERS	COMMENTS	RESULTS
Championship				

SPECIALS	LEVEL/AGE	# DANCERS	COMMENTS	RESULTS

TEAMS	LEVEL/AGE	# TEAMS	COMMENTS	RESULTS

Notes:

Feis Name: _____

Date: _____   Location: _____   Dancer #: _____

COMPETITION	LEVEL/AGE	# DANCERS	COMMENTS	RESULTS
Soft Shoe				
Hard Shoe				
Set Dance				

COMPETITION	LEVEL/AGE	# DANCERS	COMMENTS	RESULTS
Championship				

SPECIALS	LEVEL/AGE	# DANCERS	COMMENTS	RESULTS

TEAMS	LEVEL/AGE	# TEAMS	COMMENTS	RESULTS

Notes:

Feis Name: _____

Date: _____ Location: _____ Dancer #: _____

COMPETITION	LEVEL/AGE	# DANCERS	COMMENTS	RESULTS
Soft Shoe				
Hard Shoe				
Set Dance				

COMPETITION	LEVEL/AGE	# DANCERS	COMMENTS	RESULTS
Championship				

SPECIALS	LEVEL/AGE	# DANCERS	COMMENTS	RESULTS

TEAMS	LEVEL/AGE	# TEAMS	COMMENTS	RESULTS

Notes:

Feis Name: _____

Date: Location: Dancer #:

COMPETITION	LEVEL/AGE	# DANCERS	COMMENTS	RESULTS
Soft Shoe				
Hard Shoe				
Set Dance				

COMPETITION	LEVEL/AGE	# DANCERS	COMMENTS	RESULTS
Championship				

SPECIALS	LEVEL/AGE	# DANCERS	COMMENTS	RESULTS

TEAMS	LEVEL/AGE	# TEAMS	COMMENTS	RESULTS

Notes:

Feis Name: _____

Date: _____   Location: _____   Dancer #: _____

COMPETITION	LEVEL/AGE	# DANCERS	COMMENTS	RESULTS
Soft Shoe				
Hard Shoe				
Set Dance				

COMPETITION	LEVEL/AGE	# DANCERS	COMMENTS	RESULTS
Championship				

SPECIALS	LEVEL/AGE	# DANCERS	COMMENTS	RESULTS

TEAMS	LEVEL/AGE	# TEAMS	COMMENTS	RESULTS

Notes:

Feis Name: _____

Date: _____ Location: _____ Dancer #: _____

COMPETITION	LEVEL/AGE	# DANCERS	COMMENTS	RESULTS
Soft Shoe				
Hard Shoe				
Set Dance				

COMPETITION	LEVEL/AGE	# DANCERS	COMMENTS	RESULTS
Championship				

SPECIALS	LEVEL/AGE	# DANCERS	COMMENTS	RESULTS

TEAMS	LEVEL/AGE	# TEAMS	COMMENTS	RESULTS

Notes:

Feis Name: _____

Date: Location: Dancer #:

COMPETITION	LEVEL/AGE	# DANCERS	COMMENTS	RESULTS
Soft Shoe				
Hard Shoe				
Set Dance				

COMPETITION	LEVEL/AGE	# DANCERS	COMMENTS	RESULTS
Championship				

SPECIALS	LEVEL/AGE	# DANCERS	COMMENTS	RESULTS

TEAMS	LEVEL/AGE	# TEAMS	COMMENTS	RESULTS

Notes:

Feis Name: _____

Date: _____ Location: _____ Dancer #: _____

COMPETITION	LEVEL/AGE	# DANCERS	COMMENTS	RESULTS
Soft Shoe				
Hard Shoe				
Set Dance				

COMPETITION	LEVEL/AGE	# DANCERS	COMMENTS	RESULTS
Championship				

SPECIALS	LEVEL/AGE	# DANCERS	COMMENTS	RESULTS

TEAMS	LEVEL/AGE	# TEAMS	COMMENTS	RESULTS

Notes:

Feis Name: _____

Date: _____   Location: _____   Dancer #: _____

COMPETITION	LEVEL/AGE	# DANCERS	COMMENTS	RESULTS
Soft Shoe				
Hard Shoe				
Set Dance				

COMPETITION	LEVEL/AGE	# DANCERS	COMMENTS	RESULTS
Championship				

SPECIALS	LEVEL/AGE	# DANCERS	COMMENTS	RESULTS

TEAMS	LEVEL/AGE	# TEAMS	COMMENTS	RESULTS

Notes:

Feis Name: _____

Date: Location: Dancer #:

COMPETITION	LEVEL/AGE	# DANCERS	COMMENTS	RESULTS
Soft Shoe				
Hard Shoe				
Set Dance				

COMPETITION	LEVEL/AGE	# DANCERS	COMMENTS	RESULTS
Championship				

SPECIALS	LEVEL/AGE	# DANCERS	COMMENTS	RESULTS

TEAMS	LEVEL/AGE	# TEAMS	COMMENTS	RESULTS

Notes:

Feis Name: _____

Date: Location: Dancer #:

COMPETITION	LEVEL/AGE	# DANCERS	COMMENTS	RESULTS
Soft Shoe				
Hard Shoe				
Set Dance				

COMPETITION	LEVEL/AGE	# DANCERS	COMMENTS	RESULTS
Championship				

SPECIALS	LEVEL/AGE	# DANCERS	COMMENTS	RESULTS

TEAMS	LEVEL/AGE	# TEAMS	COMMENTS	RESULTS

Notes:

Feis Name: _____

Date: _____ Location: _____ Dancer #: _____

COMPETITION	LEVEL/AGE	# DANCERS	COMMENTS	RESULTS
Soft Shoe				
Hard Shoe				
Set Dance				

COMPETITION	LEVEL/AGE	# DANCERS	COMMENTS	RESULTS
Championship				

SPECIALS	LEVEL/AGE	# DANCERS	COMMENTS	RESULTS

TEAMS	LEVEL/AGE	# TEAMS	COMMENTS	RESULTS

Notes:

Feis Name: _____

Date: *Location:*   *Dancer #:*

COMPETITION	LEVEL/AGE	# DANCERS	COMMENTS	RESULTS
Soft Shoe				
Hard Shoe				
Set Dance				

COMPETITION	LEVEL/AGE	# DANCERS	COMMENTS	RESULTS
Championship				

SPECIALS	LEVEL/AGE	# DANCERS	COMMENTS	RESULTS

TEAMS	LEVEL/AGE	# TEAMS	COMMENTS	RESULTS

Notes:

Feis Name: _____

Date: _____ Location: _____ Dancer #: _____

COMPETITION	LEVEL/AGE	# DANCERS	COMMENTS	RESULTS
Soft Shoe				
Hard Shoe				
Set Dance				

COMPETITION	LEVEL/AGE	# DANCERS	COMMENTS	RESULTS
Championship				

SPECIALS	LEVEL/AGE	# DANCERS	COMMENTS	RESULTS

TEAMS	LEVEL/AGE	# TEAMS	COMMENTS	RESULTS

Notes:

Feis Name: _____

Date: *Location:*   *Dancer #:*

COMPETITION	LEVEL/AGE	# DANCERS	COMMENTS	RESULTS
Soft Shoe				
Hard Shoe				
Set Dance				

COMPETITION	LEVEL/AGE	# DANCERS	COMMENTS	RESULTS
Championship				

SPECIALS	LEVEL/AGE	# DANCERS	COMMENTS	RESULTS

TEAMS	LEVEL/AGE	# TEAMS	COMMENTS	RESULTS

Notes:

Feis Name: _____

Date: Location: Dancer #:

COMPETITION	LEVEL/AGE	# DANCERS	COMMENTS	RESULTS
Soft Shoe				
Hard Shoe				
Set Dance				

COMPETITION	LEVEL/AGE	# DANCERS	COMMENTS	RESULTS
Championship				

SPECIALS	LEVEL/AGE	# DANCERS	COMMENTS	RESULTS

TEAMS	LEVEL/AGE	# TEAMS	COMMENTS	RESULTS

Notes:

Feis Name: _____

Date: Location: Dancer #:

COMPETITION	LEVEL/AGE	# DANCERS	COMMENTS	RESULTS
Soft Shoe				
Hard Shoe				
Set Dance				

COMPETITION	LEVEL/AGE	# DANCERS	COMMENTS	RESULTS
Championship				

SPECIALS	LEVEL/AGE	# DANCERS	COMMENTS	RESULTS

TEAMS	LEVEL/AGE	# TEAMS	COMMENTS	RESULTS

Notes:

Feis Name: _____

Date: _____ Location: _____ Dancer #: _____

COMPETITION	LEVEL/AGE	# DANCERS	COMMENTS	RESULTS
Soft Shoe				
Hard Shoe				
Set Dance				

COMPETITION	LEVEL/AGE	# DANCERS	COMMENTS	RESULTS
Championship				

SPECIALS	LEVEL/AGE	# DANCERS	COMMENTS	RESULTS

TEAMS	LEVEL/AGE	# TEAMS	COMMENTS	RESULTS

Notes:

Feis Name: _____

Date: Location: Dancer #:

COMPETITION	LEVEL/AGE	# DANCERS	COMMENTS	RESULTS
Soft Shoe				
Hard Shoe				
Set Dance				

COMPETITION	LEVEL/AGE	# DANCERS	COMMENTS	RESULTS
Championship				

SPECIALS	LEVEL/AGE	# DANCERS	COMMENTS	RESULTS

TEAMS	LEVEL/AGE	# TEAMS	COMMENTS	RESULTS

Notes:

Feis Name: _____

Date: *Location:*   *Dancer #:*

COMPETITION	LEVEL/AGE	# DANCERS	COMMENTS	RESULTS
Soft Shoe				
Hard Shoe				
Set Dance				

COMPETITION	LEVEL/AGE	# DANCERS	COMMENTS	RESULTS
Championship				

SPECIALS	LEVEL/AGE	# DANCERS	COMMENTS	RESULTS

TEAMS	LEVEL/AGE	# TEAMS	COMMENTS	RESULTS

Notes:

Feis Name: _____

Date: Location: Dancer #:

COMPETITION	LEVEL/AGE	# DANCERS	COMMENTS	RESULTS
Soft Shoe				
Hard Shoe				
Set Dance				

COMPETITION	LEVEL/AGE	# DANCERS	COMMENTS	RESULTS
Championship				

SPECIALS	LEVEL/AGE	# DANCERS	COMMENTS	RESULTS

TEAMS	LEVEL/AGE	# TEAMS	COMMENTS	RESULTS

Notes:

Feis Name: _____

Date: Location: Dancer #:

COMPETITION	LEVEL/AGE	# DANCERS	COMMENTS	RESULTS
Soft Shoe				
Hard Shoe				
Set Dance				

COMPETITION	LEVEL/AGE	# DANCERS	COMMENTS	RESULTS
Championship				

SPECIALS	LEVEL/AGE	# DANCERS	COMMENTS	RESULTS

TEAMS	LEVEL/AGE	# TEAMS	COMMENTS	RESULTS

Notes:

Feis Name: _____

Date: Location: Dancer #:

COMPETITION	LEVEL/AGE	# DANCERS	COMMENTS	RESULTS
Soft Shoe				
Hard Shoe				
Set Dance				

COMPETITION	LEVEL/AGE	# DANCERS	COMMENTS	RESULTS
Championship				

SPECIALS	LEVEL/AGE	# DANCERS	COMMENTS	RESULTS

TEAMS	LEVEL/AGE	# TEAMS	COMMENTS	RESULTS

Notes:

Feis Name: _____

Date: _____   Location: _____   Dancer #: _____

COMPETITION	LEVEL/AGE	# DANCERS	COMMENTS	RESULTS
Soft Shoe				
Hard Shoe				
Set Dance				

COMPETITION	LEVEL/AGE	# DANCERS	COMMENTS	RESULTS
Championship				

SPECIALS	LEVEL/AGE	# DANCERS	COMMENTS	RESULTS

TEAMS	LEVEL/AGE	# TEAMS	COMMENTS	RESULTS

Notes:

Feis Name: _____

Date: _____ Location: _____ Dancer #: _____

COMPETITION	LEVEL/AGE	# DANCERS	COMMENTS	RESULTS
Soft Shoe				
Hard Shoe				
Set Dance				

COMPETITION	LEVEL/AGE	# DANCERS	COMMENTS	RESULTS
Championship				

SPECIALS	LEVEL/AGE	# DANCERS	COMMENTS	RESULTS

TEAMS	LEVEL/AGE	# TEAMS	COMMENTS	RESULTS

Notes:

Feis Name: _____

Date: _____ Location: _____ Dancer #: _____

COMPETITION	LEVEL/AGE	# DANCERS	COMMENTS	RESULTS
Soft Shoe				
Hard Shoe				
Set Dance				

COMPETITION	LEVEL/AGE	# DANCERS	COMMENTS	RESULTS
Championship				

SPECIALS	LEVEL/AGE	# DANCERS	COMMENTS	RESULTS

TEAMS	LEVEL/AGE	# TEAMS	COMMENTS	RESULTS

Notes:

Feis Name: _____

Date: _____ Location: _____ Dancer #: _____

COMPETITION	LEVEL/AGE	# DANCERS	COMMENTS	RESULTS
Soft Shoe				
Hard Shoe				
Set Dance				

COMPETITION	LEVEL/AGE	# DANCERS	COMMENTS	RESULTS
Championship				

SPECIALS	LEVEL/AGE	# DANCERS	COMMENTS	RESULTS

TEAMS	LEVEL/AGE	# TEAMS	COMMENTS	RESULTS

Notes: